RECKLESS SIMPLICITY

poems by

Robin Lee

Finishing Line Press
Georgetown, Kentucky

RECKLESS SIMPLICITY

Editor: Christen Kincaid

Cover Art: Elizabeth Blank

Author Photo: Robin Lee

Cover Design: Elizabeth Maines

Printed in the USA on acid-free paper.
Order online: www.finishinglinepress.com
also available on amazon.com

Author inquiries and mail orders:
Finishing Line Press
P. O. Box 1626
Georgetown, Kentucky 40324
U. S. A.

Table of Contents

For my Mother and Father
and my Brothers four

QUEST/IONS

How do I
float?

Let go

Keep my bike
right?

Push harder

When to
flex,

when to
flow

Questions
that

we don't
outgrow

RABBIT FEEND

Twilight
in the freshly shorn
suburban grass
it's time for the
children to go in
now

Set down food
for the rabbit feends
we have been
playing with
rub their warm
furry tummies
and to bed

Slow sing solemn
song
children's voices sing:

"Oh rabbit feend
Oh rabbit feend
North is north
And south is south
Oh rabbit feend"

As the song chants on
one by one we
fall away

Kiss and
depart
the deep green
dark

kiss
and goodnight.

SUGAR DONUTS

white icing sugar
coating cake so
white

bite

the sweet shock
swells and
falls off

the cool spring air
the lake and the ducks

my mother and me
sharing a snack
together

my brother and father
are not with us I
don't know why

just my mother and
me and the outside
surrounding

the air and the birds
and the sense of
two as one

having fun with no
thought of after or
before

like icing sugar on
white, white
cake

the moment grows, shines a
while, becomes happiness
remembered

GIBBOUS MOON

No sooner full than
falls away. Wax to
wane a porous
trace.

And Britain's coast
still undefined. The
fractal fact in
place.

Still day to day we
walk our world,
certainties
secure,

its giddy ride to
cold and still
sufficiently
obscure.

BANSURI

Over the drone,
the tabla dancing,
the bamboo bansuri

sounds.

Reels and keens,
whispers and
floats—

a wind instrument
where pitch
must be

found

in and around
the
notes.

Drama ensues: can
wildness be
tamed,

aligned with
man's
aims?

For a time it
can seem
so,

in the end must
be let
go.

FIRST SERVICES, SANDY HOOK

December 16, 2012

The patter
shatters

Again and
again

This ever recurring
pattern of

rain

Can we span the
pain?

Can we seek the
change?

Can we meet Spring's
range?

MOUNT RAINIER APPROACHED FROM THE NORTH

Suddenly seen–great rock
mass, snow white
sheen

The world dispersed,
of course, in
dream

POEMS AFTER THREE PAINTINGS BY DAVID BERG

I.   RING

Begin with the flame, the sky-stolen fire,
rending the flesh of the newly owned
night. Draw back to skin of bodies
surrounding, flame circled out and then
flared into sight. Maddened ecstatic the
ring of the dancers loses itself into self
into flame. Loses itself until both share
one name.

II.   WOMAN AND CENTAUR

All that compels the two together serves
as well to drive them apart. The centaur on the
left, the woman on the right. He seen in profile,
she from behind. Both blocked in boldly the lines
darker gray carved into blue-and-gray painterly slate.

The centaur bears down his hooves raised in
passion. Yet seems to be trying to slow his approach.
The woman we see has two sets of arms. One pair turns
her yearning towards him, the other pair turns her
sadly away.

And so to today—cave painting, mythos, the new brought
to bear. Those things about which we humanly care are
not without their inverse owing. Trying to find required
wild mind is all of the best we can be.

III.   THE SILVER AND THE GOLD

Gas-shrouded mountains beautiful still.
The silver-blue question we cannot kill.
So many layers, it seems, between
the thing that is felt and the thing that is seen.

Hating ourselves for all we have sold
we puncture its surface with stakes of gold.

THE SPADEFOOT TOAD

Consider the toad.
The spadefoot
toad.

As one they sound,
baffle foes with
common

sync.

A jet flies by,
perturbs this
link:

hawks swoop
down, take
toads

exposed—Nature
opposed, and
we don't

blink.

HURRICANE

Wind so strong
seagulls
suspend

The ocean whips to creamy
froth as we walk out
along the pier

My son age five
a mix of fear
delight,

his small self pressed against
the wind which steals my
voice from him

Watching my mind recalls
a time when I, his age or
nearly, was so buffeted

My brother and I ecstatic in
autumn Toronto running
through wind as thick

and strong as
ocean
waves

Pagan barbarous the taste of
madness on our lips we
pressed the bounds of
our suburban yard

while puzzled parents secured
our home against the
hurricane
incoming

Then called us in
from wildness wind
to rooms warm and
familiar

But in my skin
a smaller wind had
kindled. And now and then

since then to now inside and
familiar things seem
somehow less than
real

Once again I watch my son
watch him ravished by
the wind and wish

for him as well a small
storm kindled in the
skin

May he also never
quite come
in

ON A PHOTOGRAPH OF BILL EVANS TAKEN IN THE LATE FIFTIES

Have you heard the music?
Filigree of steel fine spun one
web of sound so woven that countersong
and song itself swoop and soar and
twirl and bound amid harmonic arches set
in ground and inner voices whisper soft, as
moments forward flow, till time is tricked
outside itself until the music's close.

Have you seen the picture?
Grand piano shot from above, its black back fills
most of the frame. What space remains displays
a pale black-suited acolyte of jazz—perched
on edge of piano bench, hunched over almost double,
head bowed low his arms stretched out his fingers
tracing web-like patterns on the keys.

Is he reaching to the huge black mass for solace from
some pain? Is he bent towards its darkness in an
attitude of praying? Or is he rather reaching out
and conjuring its keys—conjuring to hold surrounding
darknesses at bay.

For himself and through his art as well for you and me,
conjuring to hold surrounding darknesses at bay.

THE BARGAIN

Okay, I've got the secret
identity.

Now how about those
superpowers?

PARADISE, PARADISE (A SHOE SIZE LOST)

Lost a whole shoe size the
other day

Ten to nine I think it
was

Still, it simplifies
parking.

Saw a girl sidestep
cautiously

Small streams of sidewalk
wash

Her shoe size seemed
secure,

or not. There are many tabled
questions:

Of force majeure invoked,
then dropped,

Of certain sizes skewing
south,

Though parking still informs
the lot.

ZUGZWANG or **ME AND MRS. ROBINSON**

Zug: to pull or move
Zwang: to oblige or force

Hearty thanks to the German
language and its glorious
compound nouns!

Without them how else
could I express my
inner self-

weltschmerz leavened only
by random flashes of
schadenfreude.

And the word I believe
coined specifically
for me:

Zugzwang

That implacable chess
moment when your
opponent

has limited your
available
moves

to those that harm
position, cost
men.

Every way you look
at it you
lose.

WHAT WE FORGET TO KNOW

(after Howard Nemerov)

White with black-tipped wings
and tail, yellow-shaded head
and predatory beak, the
gannet

scans the sea below, locks
onto prey, plunges cold
Atlantic depths,
splashes

ocean into sheer scrim that
catches sun, reveals the
hidden spectral stuff
of light.

A sight that lasts an
instant only, but an
instant is
enough.

SHOCK KILLS RARE RHINO: HEAD STUCK IN GATE
San Francisco Chronicle

A rare Indian rhinoceros
apparently died of shock
after getting its head stuck
overnight
in an 18-inch opening
in a metal gate
at the Los Angeles Zoo
officials said yesterday

"It couldn't have been
more bizarre"
the Zoo Director said

Rhada, 21-years-old, had given
birth to two calves,
including a 2-year-old
male that was
with her
in the pen when
she died

Rhinos generally live
to be about
40

It goes unsaid but
one may presume
the pen
met all the standards
men determine
sufficient to safely

hem
a rhino

"It couldn't have been more
bizarre"

We are permitted to think
that everyone's best
efforts were
involved to solve
the dilemma of
containing the huge
mysterious beast
primitive and beautiful

And so it is
and so it goes
and on and on and
on it seems
the dark mysterious
primitive dreams

scream

against the well thought
out and reasoned
pen

against the best
intentions
of men

CONSIDER THE WIND

When all else fails
consider the wind

Leaves a breeze
a snub of pain

And then, perhaps,
consider the rain

A wash away of
what remains

And finally, then,
consider the sun

Everything
undone

Forward path
begun

LIFE AS CROSSWORD

The more you
suss it out

the simpler it
becomes

then soon, too soon
it seems,

the puzzle's simply
done

RED ROCKET

I read it in the paper:

McDonald's will pay a
four-million-dollar fine
for failing to report injuries
suffered by children playing on
Big Mac Climber jungle gyms.

The offending equipment will be
removed and softer surfaces
and safer angles installed
to forestall subsequent
similar events.

I hope no one was badly hurt.

Still, perhaps, a short sigh
for the banished Climber
is not fully out of place.
For I recall a similar structure
I played on as a boy.

A steel skeleton spacecraft
painted primary hues—horizontal
blue pipes ladder you into its red tube body,
orange angled metal flame behind, and
yellow capsule-sphere in front.

And, of course, a disk-like steering
wheel. RED ROCKET I dub it in my mind.
And while I play there often with my friends
and brothers, when I play there alone
it is most mine.

After school, as evening falls,
several nights a week I strive to
rule the intricacies of my
space vessel. It is not an
easy task.

For play structures of the day
fail to take account of a
nine-year-old's propensity to
misjudge a jump. To overstate an
act of balance.

It is a high-stakes game. And so it is
with bruised arms and sore legs I negotiate
my red metal adversary. And slowly, through
the weeks, achieve a heady sense
of mastery.

Then—mind and muscles newly tuned—
I space walk the perimeter of my craft, dangle
head down from yellow capsule, swing legs
between bars into entrance hatch, and
resume my signal journey.

Sole commander of RED ROCKET,
intrepid explorer of space, my skill and
fame forged in the crucible of design now
deemed potentially injurious to
children.

Several years ago, on a visit home,
I saw RED ROCKET was gone.
It is joined now in its politically incorrect
pasture by the much maligned
Big Mac Climber.

Will children, enjoying the softer
surfaces and safer angles of new and
improved play structures, find in them
stirring challenge? In a cell-phone-buffered
cyber world is there any place
for space?

I don't know. But angled orange metal
flames still shimmer in the distance.
May they always glow.

THE SHORE

Blue and black rock half-buried
in sand,

near to the shore the size of
my fist.

Ocean waves rhythmically cover
and bathe,

green and gold glints shimmer
sun kissed.

Not to be touched not to
be moved,

not to be framed exposed
and caught.

Turn and slowly walk back to
the car,

you find that you have what
you sought.

YOU CAN'T HAVE EVERYTHING

Like the poet said:
you can't have everything,

but you can have

the too cold beer on the too hot day
the narcotic purr of the cat
the pleasure of your child's pleasure

the casual few words exchanged with your wife
that limn long years of love

the glow of a poem well written that lasts
most of the day

the self-erasing splurge of sex

the sense of connection when your words
slower, sadder improve Chopin
as played by your son

And Tom Waits on his new CD

"I'm gonna take it with me
when I go…"

Take it with me when I go.

JOY

A day full no
record
cast

of time's lapse,
of first
and

last. Instants
pass—grasp
what

lasts

Robin has been writing poetry for many years. In 2104 Finishing Line Press published his first poetry chapbook, *The Live Long Day*. Both this book and *Reckless Simplicity* have been featured on Bay Area radio station KPFA's *Cover to Cover*. Professionally, Robin works in motion picture post-production as a Picture Editor. He lives in Marin County, California.

www.ingramcontent.com/pod-product-compliance
Lightning Source LLC
LaVergne TN
LVHW091234080426
835509LV00009B/1274